D1234755

THIS STRANGE JOY

THIS
STRANGE
JOY

Selected Poems of Sandro Penna

Translated from the Italian by W. S. Di Piero

Ohio State University Press : Columbus

All of the poems by Sandro Penna that make up this selected edition were originally published in Italian by Garzanti Editore of Milan in the first edition of Penna's *Tutte le poesie* of 1970 and *Stranezze* of 1976. They are reprinted here in the original Italian with the permission of Garzanti Editore, which has also authorized publication of the English translations by W. S. Di Piero.

Library of Congress Cataloging in Publication Data

Penna, Sandro.
  This strange joy.

  English and Italian.
  Includes bibliographical references.
  I. Title.
PQ4835.E47A24   1982   851'.914   81-22288
ISBN 0-8142-0328-0   AACR2

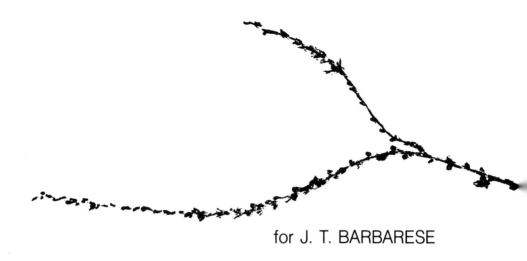

for J. T. BARBARESE

CONTENTS

Foreword   xv

PART ONE

"La vita . . . è ricordarsi di un risveglio"   2
"Life . . . is remembering a sad"   3

"Mi avevano lasciato solo"   4
"They'd left me alone"   5

Autunno   6
Autumn   7

"Notte: sogno di sparse"   6
"Night: dream of scattered"   7

"Nel sonno incerto sogno ancora un poco"   8
"In my fitful sleep I'll dream a little longer"   9

"Se la notte d'estate cede un poco"   8
"When the summer night begins to yield"   9

"Basta all'amore degli adolescenti"   10
"Adolescents in love need only"   11

"Se dietro la finestra illuminata"   10
"If a boy sleeping behind"   11

Nuotatore   12
Swimmer   13

Cimitero di campagna   12
Country Cemetery   13

Città   14
City   15

Falsa primavera   16
False Spring   17

Sera nel giardino   18
Evening in the Park   19

Scuola 18
School 19

"Le nere scale della mia taverna" 20
"All tangled with wind you walk" 21

Favola 20
Fable 21

Fantasia per un inizio di primavera 22
Fantasy for a Spring Beginning 23

"Sotto il cielo di aprile la mia pace" 24
"Under the April sky the peace I feel" 25

Il balcone 26
The Balcony 27

"Le stelle sono immobili nel cielo" 26
"The stars don't move in the sky" 27

"Già mi parla l'autunno. Al davanzale" 28
"Autumn speaks to me already. At the dark" 29

"Esco dal mio lavoro tutto pieno" 28
"I leave my job filled" 29

"Se sono vuoti gli alberi e il gennaio" 30
"When the trees are bare and January" 31

Torre 30
Tower 31

"Eccoli gli operai sul prato verde" 32
"Look at the workers on the green field" 33

Interno 32
Interior 33

"È pur dolce il ritrovarsi" 34
"It's also good to find yourself" 35

"Era il settembre. Riandava la gente" 36
"It was September. People walked" 37

Il vegetale 36
Greenery 37

"La veneta piazzetta"   38
"The small Venetian piazza"   39

"Io vivere vorrei addormentato"   38
"I'd like to live falling to sleep"   39

Paesaggio   40
Landscape   41

"Mentre noi siamo qui, fra consuete"   40
"While we're here, buried among"   41

"Le porte del mondo non sanno"   42
"The doors of the world don't know"   43

"I pini solitari lungo il mare"   44
"The solitary pines along the empty"   45

"Era l'alba su i colli, e gli animali"   46
"Dawn on the hills, and the animals"   47

"Quando tornai al mare di una volta"   48
"When I went back to the sea I once knew"   49

La tomba del padre   48
The Father's Tomb   49

Fine di stagione   50
Season's End   51

"La luna di settembre su la buia"   52
"September moon on the dark valley"   53

"Quando la luce piange sulle strade"   52
"When light weeps on the streets"   53

"Un bicchiere di latte ed una piazza"   54
"A glass of milk and a piazza"   55

"Un giorno che alla terra abbandonavo"   54
"One day when I surrendered to the earth"   55

"Deserto è il fiume. E tu lo sai che basta"   56
"The river's deserted. And you know"   57

"Non era la città dove la sera"   56
"It wasn't the city where I used to sing"   57

La sera   58
The Evening   59

La tempesta   58
The Tempest   59

"Non ami le pareti della tua"   60
"You don't love the walls of your"   61

"Con un rapido vezzo hai liberato"   60
"One neat flick freed your"   61

"Era per la città quasi un comune"   62
"In the city he seemed an ordinary"   63

"Viene l'alba d'estate. Oh prima luce"   62
"The summer dawn rises. O early light"   63

"La mia vita è monotona, se arde"   64
"My life is monotonous when quiet"   65

"La semplice poesia forse discende"   64
"Maybe plain and easy poetry happens"   65

"Malinconia d'amore, dove resta"   64
"Love's sadness, where the boy's"   65

"L'insonnia delle rondini. L'amico"   66
"The swallows' insomnia. My quiet"   67

"L'accusato non ha se non parole"   66
"The accused has only words"   67

"Immobile nel sole la campagna"   66
"Motionless in sunlight, the landscape"   67

"Forse invecchio, se ho fatto un lungo viaggio"   68
"Maybe I'm getting old, staying seated"   69

"Qualcuno vi parlava e voi rispondevate"   70
"Someone was talking to you and you were answering"   71

"Abbandonarsi all'onda delle sensazioni"   70
"Surrendering to the wave of feelings"   71

"Amavo ogni cosa nel mondo. E non avevo"   72
"I loved everything in the world. And all I had"   73

"Lumi del cimitero, non mi dite"   72
"Cemetery lights, don't tell me"   73

"Ero solo nel mondo, o il mondo aveva"   74
"I was alone in the world, or did the world"   75

"Sedere a una tavola ignota"   74
"To sit at a strange table"   75

"Ditemi, grandi alberi sognanti"   76
"Tell me, you great dreaming trees"   77

"Ero solo e seduto. La mia storia"   76
"I was sitting alone. I entrusted"   77

"L'estate se ne andò senza rumore"   78
"Summer made no noise when it left"   79

"Un uomo già cantava nel suo buio"   78
"A man was singing in his darkness"   79

"Il treno tarderà di almeno un'ora"   80
"The train will be at least an hour late"   81

PART TWO

"Felice chi è diverso"   84
"Happy the man who is different"   85

"E poi son solo. Resta"   84
"And so I'm alone. Alone"   85

"Viaggiava per la terra"   86
"He walked the earth"   87

"Non è la timidezza che tu celi forse un sogno"   86
"Isn't the shyness you hide perhaps a puzzled"   87

"Qui è la cara città dove la notte"   88
"This is the good city where the dead"   89

"Il fanciullo magretto torna a casa"   88
"A skinny young boy is on his way home"   89

"Un po' di pace è già nella campagna"   90
"There's still a little peace in the country"   91

"Dacci la gioia di conoscer bene"   90
"Grant us the joy of knowing well"   91

"Se l'inverno comincia sulle calde"   92
"Winter begins and a smell"   93

"Un dì la vita mia era beata"   92
"My life one day was blessed"   93

"Con il cielo coperto e con l'aria monotona"   94
"With the sky overcast and the bleak flat air"   95

"Come è forte il rumore dell'alba"   94
"Dawn makes so much noise"   95

"Mi ridestava la voce"   96
"I was roused again"   97

"Sul campo aperto giuocano al pallone"   96
"They're playing ball on the wide field"   97

"È bello lavorare"   98
"It's good to work"   99

"Se desolato io cammino ... dietro"   98
"If I go for a walk, dejected ... behind"   99

"Sole con luna, mare con foreste"   100
"Sun with moon, sea with forests"   101

"'Lasciami andare se già spunta l'alba' "   100
" 'Let me go, it's nearly dawn' "   101

"Amico, sei lontano. E la tua vita"   102
"Friend, you're far away. And your life"   103

Donna in tram   102
Woman in a Streetcar   103

"Nel chiuso lago, sola, senza vento"   104
"My boat drifts, windless, alone"   105

"Guarirai. Si odono i treni"   104
"You'll recover. You can hear the trains"   105

"Lungo è il tragitto in autobus. Anche"   106
"The bus trip's long. Even though"   107

"Amore, gioventù, liete parole"   106
"Love, youth, sweet words"   107

"La mia poesia non sarà"   108
"My poetry won't be"   109

"Il fanciullo che ascolta nei libri"   108
"The boy listening to songs"   109

"Mi adagio nel mattino"   110
"I lie down in the spring"   111

"Voglio credere ancora in te, Marcello"   110
"I want to go on believing in you, Marcello"   111

"Vivere è per amare qualche cosa"   112
"We live to love something"   113

Mattino   112
Morning   113

"L'ombra di una nuvola leggera"   114
"The shadow of a drifting cloud"   115

"Di febbraio a Milano"   114
"That February in Milan"   115

"Tutto il giorno passai coi contadini"   116
"I spent all day with the peasants"   117

"Indifeso fervore. Brilla sul ciglio"   116
"Unguarded passion. Burlesque glamor"   117

Moralisti   118
Moralists   119

"Sempre fanciulli nelle mie poesie"   118
"Always boys in my poems"   119

"Oh il lamento arrugginito"   118
"O the sad rusty song"   119

"Fuoco nero fra schiuma di mare"   120
"Black fire on sea foam"   121

"Sempre affacciato a una finestra io sono"   120
"I'm always standing by a window"   121

"Imbruna l'aria, e il lume"   122
"The air darkens and daylight"   123

"Sulla riva del fiume ancora brillano"   124
"Bodies of naked men in the distance"   125

Il viaggio   124
The Journey   125

Alla luna   126
To the Moon   127

Pianto   126
Crying   127

"Voi già sognate il caffelatte. Io la mia tazza"   128
"While you're still dreaming of your morning coffee"   129

" 'Poeta esclusivo d'amore' "   128
" 'A love poet exclusively' "   129

"Talvolta, camminando per la via"   130
"Sometimes, walking down a street"   131

"Alfio che un treno porta assai lontano"   130
"A train taking Alfio far away"   131

"Non c'è più quella grazia fulminante"   132
"No more of that lightning grace"   133

Cronache di primavera   132
Spring News   133

"Forse sull'erba verde un dì nasceva"   134
"I think my secret story was born one day"   135

"E poi come una mosca"   134
"And then like a fly"   135

FOREWORD

In 1973, when I was doing my first translations of Sandro Penna's poems, I hoped to meet Penna and show him the results of my work. I tried to arrange an introduction through intermediaries, one of them an old friend of the poet, but the meeting never came about. I was told that Penna, then in failing health and more reclusive than ever, refused to see anyone except a few close friends. He continued to live an extremely private, guarded life, aloof from public literary affairs. Not long afterward, in 1977, Penna died in Rome, where he had lived most of his adult years. He was seventy-one.

Penna was perhaps the least visible, the least public, of important Italian poets, yet his reputation as a distinguished lyric poet seemed unquestioned among Italian men of letters. In conversations with writers and critics, I was often told that any understanding of modern Italian poetry would be incomplete without consideration of Sandro Penna. As early as 1958 Pier Paolo Pasolini was already insisting that there were few serious readers of poetry who did not esteem Penna's work.[1] Whereas most of his contemporaries had managed to elude poverty (usually by means of what Eugenio Montale has called "second occupations," such as university teaching, translating, and journalism), Penna's circumstances remained minimal even in his last days, a fact much proclaimed and lamented by the Italian press after the poet's death. For most of his life he subsisted on a series of sporadic, inconsequential jobs—bookstore clerk, proofreader, vendor—though he never had to settle for the kind of work common among the very poor: "I never shined shoes, cut hair, cooked, or washed dishes."[2] Because his poetry remained so remote from his daily nonliterary routines, it seemed to some readers all the more purified.

Penna's poetry is so unlike most modern Italian poetry that some commentators refer to him as an island mysteriously set apart from the main traditions. This is not entirely accurate. When Penna published his first poems in the thirties, the most prominent literary movement was hermeticism, with which he is still sometimes mistakenly associated. Rejecting the lush sensualism of D'Annunzio and the explosive rancor of the futurists, the hermetics sought a poetry that would make immediate the most intense and desperate internal states. Their tone was contemplative but not easeful or languid, hierophantic but not pompous, authoritative but not bullying. They favored a sustained epigrammatic form that frequently turned on a fusion of two disparate terms. Ungaretti's famous one-line poem is an extreme example: "D'altri diluvi una colomba ascolto" ("I listen to a dove from other floods.") Metaphor became a gesture toward recondite correspondences, self-enclosed, sealed. A poem thus became the most private of rooms.

Penna, even in his early poems, was more declarative and ecstatic, plainer and more direct. Hermetic metaphor held little attraction. In an interview shortly before his death, he reiterated his detachment from, and dislike for, certain poets—Ungaretti, Quasimodo ("He wrote one good line"),[3] and Montale—whose voices helped define the hermetic mode of speech. And indeed one finds very little trace in his work of Ungaretti's spare, carved diction or of Montale's iridescent figures of speech. So although one may assume that he was aware of the poetry then being written (and much written about) and that was shaping the modernist tradition in Italy, and although he shared with the hermetics their urgent personal tone of voice, Penna for the most part followed his own lead, answered his own literary needs.

There were, however, two poets whose influence on Penna was direct and crucial. Guido Gozzano (1883–1916) was the leading figure of a group of poets active at the beginning of the century called I crepuscolari, "Poets of the Twilight." Gozzano made ordinary life in all its humble and banal elements the main subject of poetry. He wrote of le piccole cose, little things, for their own sake, without conscious symbolic shadowing. Penna's poetry, too, fixes on ordinary things and events, and it speaks occasionally in the tones of world-weariness, of exhaustion and ennui, that hum throughout Gozzano's work. Gozzano's world, however, is resolutely unidealized and nontranscendent, whereas Penna restlessly looks for the divine light that charges from within the most ordinary things. But the existential position from which Gozzano speaks—and of which the following lines are, I think, representative—is also the initial situation out of which some of Penna's poems emerge:

> Non vivo. Solo, gelido, in disparte
> sorrido e guardo vivere me stesso.

I don't live. Alone, cold, apart,
I smile and watch myself living.

("I colloqui" / "Conversations")[4]

A more immediate and constant influence on Penna was Umberto Saba (1883–1957). It was Saba who helped publish Penna's first poems, and the two remained friends for a long time. They shared a certain pride in standing apart from literary trends and movements. Both took personality as a recurrent poetic subject and nurtured a brooding, self-conscious solitariness as the ground and matter of poetic speech. Both wrote numerous poems about the yearning to commune with others, to reach out toward a life perceived in the distance.[5] But temperamental self-containment frequently, and naturally, denied them participation in that world of others. The result, for both poets, is a deep melancholy of detachment. Saba's leisurely and supple diction is suited to sustained lyrical meditation. Penna, on the other hand, seldom engages any kind of rhetorical investigation of melancholy; his poems are more compacted than Saba's, and their impassioned solipsism is more concentrated and insistent.[6]

If Penna is an island in modern Italian poetry, then, he is one in an archipelago that itself lies within sight of larger continental masses. Echoes carry far, and we can hear in Penna's lyrics the epigrammatic voice favored by the hermetics. And, like them, he adjusts his own kind of antieloquence to serve his aspiration of elevating quotidian human experience to the threshold of the unsayable. Penna has said that his perfect poems are his shortest, those of two or three or four lines. Within these confines he articulates a moment of sensation in which even the most inconsequential experience may become at once the most rarefied:

I lie down in the spring
morning. I feel
disordered dawns sprouting
inside me. I no longer know
whether I'm dying or being born.

An instant's illumination suffices for what, in another poem, he calls "la semplice poesia," plain and easy poetry.

It is impossible to distinguish Penna's cult of the instantaneous from his unrelenting solipsism. Taken together they result in a narrow range of subject and tone. Even his eroticism—in interviews he spoke quite openly of his *pederastia*—is frequently an expression of sullen self-absorption. It is a commonplace but perhaps needs to be said that Penna, like the ancient models of Sappho, Ibykos, and Anacreon, to whom he is clearly indebted, speaks only in the presence of what moves him and does not sing in the presence of what does not. His *opere* constitute a chronicle of privileged instants, heightened occasions. The external materials or props remain constant: an open or lighted window, an empty room or street, a grassy field or crowded train, sunlight, rivers, boys. Each poem tells a slightly different turning toward the familiar world, toward normalized experience made suddenly extraordinary by the apparition of a face, a voice, a rustling of trees, a change of light.

One should not go to Penna expecting a vision of historical process or swarming physical details. His minimalist lyrics at times seem about to disintegrate and vanish into their own rich, recurrent abstractions: adjectives like *lieto, lieve, dolce, bello*; verbs like *sognare, sentire, volere, nascere, sapere*; and the noun, omnipresent, *amore*. Penna's simple, elusive language remains bound, however, to the most immediate kinds of experience. The poems allow us to become familiar with a few (only a few) of his personal habits, most of all his long walks in favorite places, in fields, parks, and working-class neighborhoods.

More important than his subject matter is Penna's mode of vision. He stares intensely at what he sees, but not to clarify the object or dramatize its details; rather, his gaze isolates the object or momentary scene in order to disclose the god, Eros, who animates all things. Over and over again Penna celebrates love in its divine and profane forms. Cesare Garboli has written that "for Penna everything remains divine, and everything remains carnal."[7] In his many poems (over four hundred published in his lifetime) he tried to achieve, through concentration on the instantaneous, a purified utterance that might somehow snap and transcend time's definitions. In one poem he announces his ambition: "My poetry will hurl its strength / and lose itself in the infinite." Elsewhere he regards his work in less lofty terms: "Joining words to men was the brief / adequate gift the gods gave me." Such aspiration, given the formal limitations Penna imposes on himself, becomes at times a liability and results in preciosity or obscurantism.

Penna's method may be problematical in a time when many readers are unaccustomed to, or indisposed toward, abstract lyric sentiment, such as "the solitary pines won't see / my death dancing with love." And his homoerotic lyrics, chaste and dreamy as they are, do not indulge in glamorous pronouncement. Whatever the expressed object of his desire—person, landscape, community—Penna is most concerned with articulating the melancholy, at times ecstatic, turns of assimilation and exclusion, of absorption (one of his key words) and estrangement.

Garboli has commented on Penna's very arbitrary arrangement of his poems: they simply follow "one after another, without obeying any 'higher systems' of order."[8] Consequently, the poems are nearly impossible to date. In assembling this collection I have used as my texts the first edition of *Tutte le poesie* (Garzanti, 1970) and *Stranezze* (Garzanti, 1976). Part 1 of my text is drawn from the first two sections of *Tutte le poesie* ("Poesie 1927–1938" and "Poesie inedite 1927–1955"); part 2 draws on the remaining five sections of that work, plus fourteen poems from *Stranezze*. With only a few exceptions I have followed the sequence of poems as they appear in the Italian texts.

I wish to thank E. V. Griffith, editor of *Poetry Now*, for his constant enthusiasm and support while this translation was in progress. I am grateful to Charles Klopp not only for his corrections and criticisms of an earlier version of the manuscript but also for his suggestion that it be expanded in order to give a broader view of Penna's work. My greatest debt is to William Arrowsmith, whose candid and scrupulous criticism of every poem forced me to reexamine my strategies and, as a result, to revise and improve each lyric.

This project is partially supported by a grant from the Illinois Arts Council, a state agency.

W. S. Di Piero

1. Pier Paolo Pasolini, *Passione e ideologia* (Milan: Garzanti, 1973), p. 405.

2. Quoted in *L'Unità* (Rome), 24 January 1977, p. 3.

3. *Il Messagero* (Rome), 24 January 1977, p. 3.

4. Guido Gozzano, *Le poesie* (Milan: Garzanti, 1971), p. 78 (translation mine).

5. "In Penna there's an initial renunciation of complete joy, of communal action with others, which coincides with the renunciation of the consciousness of sin" (Pasolini, *Passione e ideologia*, p. 403).

6. "[Penna] decided to win his own results by a quicker and more direct route; he did not pursue the long narrative route taken by Saba. Penna is content with the more immediate and instantaneously emotive effect" (Gianni Pozzi, *La poesia italiana del novecento* [Turin: Einaudi, 1965], p. 316).

7. Cesare Garboli, in "Postfazione" to Sandro Penna's *Stranezze* (Milan: Garzanti, 1976), p. 135.

8. Ibid., p. 132.

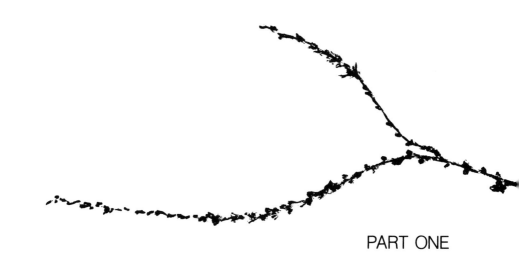

PART ONE

La vita . . . è ricordarsi di un risveglio
triste in un treno all'alba: aver veduto
fuori la luce incerta: aver sentito
nel corpo rotto la malinconia
vergine e aspra dell'aria pungente.

Ma ricordarsi la liberazione
improvvisa è più dolce: a me vicino
un marinaio giovane: l'azzurro
e il bianco della sua divisa, e fuori
un mare tutto fresco di colore.

Life . . . is remembering a sad
waking in a train at dawn, seeing
the tentative light outside, feeling
in the broken body the bitter virgin
sorrow of the piercing air.

But remembering the sudden release
is sweeter, a young sailor
beside me, the blue and white
of his uniform, and outside
a sea all crisp with color.

Mi avevano lasciato solo
nella campagna, sotto
la pioggia fina, solo.
Mi guardavano muti
meravigliati
i nudi pioppi: soffrivano
della mia pena: pena
di non saper chiaramente . . .

E la terra bagnata
e i neri altissimi monti
tacevano vinti. Sembrava
che un dio cattivo
avesse con un sol gesto
tutto pietrificato.

E la pioggia lavava quelle pietre.

They'd left me alone
in the country, alone
in the misty rain.
The naked poplars, mute
and amazed,
watched me, suffered
my pain, this pain
of not knowing clearly . . .

And the wet earth
and towering black mountains
were silent, subdued. As if
some bad god
with a single gesture
had petrified everything.

And the rain washed those stones.

AUTUNNO

Il vento ti ha lasciata un'eco chiara,
nei sensi, delle cose ch'ài vedute
—confuse—il giorno. All'apparir del sonno
difenderti non sai: un crisantemo,
un lago tremulo e una esigua fila
d'alberi gialloverdi sotto il sole.

Notte: sogno di sparse
finestre illuminate.
Sentir la chiara voce
dal mare. Da un amato
libro veder parole
sparire . . . —Oh stelle in corsa
l'amore della vita!

AUTUMN

The wind has left with you
a clear echo of things—confused
things—you've seen by day. You can't
protect yourself from looming sleep: a chrysanthemum,
a quivering lake, a trace of trees
yellowgreen in the sunlight.

Night: dream of scattered
windows lighting.
Hearing the clear voice
from the sea. Watching words
in a favorite book
disappear . . . O stars turning
love of life!

Nel sonno incerto sogno ancora un poco.
È forse giorno. Dalla strada il fischio
di un pescatore e la sua voce calda.
A lui risponde una voce assonnata.

Trasalire dei sensi—con le vele,
fuori, nel vento?—Io sogno ancora un poco.

Se la notte d'estate cede un poco
su la riva del mare sorgeranno
—nati in silenzio come i suoi colori—
uomini nudi e leggeri che vanno.

Ma come il vento muove il mare, muovono
anche, gridando, gli uomini le barche.

Sorge sull'ultimo sudore il sole.

In my fitful sleep I'll dream a little longer.
Maybe it's day. From the street a fisherman's
whistle, his warm voice.
A sleepy voice answers him.

Senses rocking . . . with sails,
outside, in the wind? . . . I'll dream a little longer.

— PN 24

When the summer night begins to yield
at the sea's edge, men will emerge
—born in silence like the colors of the sea—
naked and buoyant, leaving.

But like the wind that moves the sea, so
the men, shouting, move their boats.

The sun rises on their sweat.

Basta all'amore degli adolescenti
sentirsi possedere
dal sole entro la sabbia calda immoti.

Tutto è così. Non viene un forte vento
a rovesciare la calma accecante.

La sera, all'ombra della cattedrale,
con gridi e gridi giuocano i fanciulli.
Ma nel silenzio è inutile la voce

anche delle campane.

Se dietro la finestra illuminata
dorme un fanciullo, nella notte estiva,
e sognerà . . .
                    Passa veloce un treno
e va lontano.
                    Il mare è come prima.

Adolescents in love need only
feel possessed by the sun
where they lie buried under the hot sand.

Everything's like that. No strong wind
comes to unsettle the blinding calm.

Evenings, in the shadow of the cathedral,
the kids play, yelling and screaming.
But even the voice of the bells

is pointless in the silence.

—PN 30

If a boy sleeping behind
the lighted window on a summer night
begins to dream . . .
                        A train rushes past
on into the distance.
                        The sea is the same as always.

NUOTATORE

Dormiva . . . ?
Poi si tolse e si stirò.
Guardò con occhi lenti l'acqua. Un guizzo
il suo corpo.
Così lasciò la terra.

CIMITERO DI CAMPAGNA

Fra la gioia dei grilli
oscure fiaccole.

E in alto le stelle.

Al giovane cuore
la riposata ridda
delle solari
gesta del giorno.

Ma un'ansia i ridenti occhi
già turba
al fanciullo venuto
per gioia con me.

SWIMMER

Was he sleeping?
                    Then he undressed and stretched.
He watched the water, slowly. His body
wriggling.
                    That was how he left the earth.

COUNTRY CEMETERY

In the joy of the crickets
dark torches.

The stars overhead.

In his young heart
the quiet reeling
of the day's
sunlit deeds.

But something anxious
troubles the laughing eyes
of the boy who came
with me, for joy.

CITTA

Livida alba, io sono senza dio.

Visi assonnati vanno per le vie
sepolti sotto fasci d'erbe diacce.
Gridano al freddo vuoto i venditori.

Albe più dense di colori vidi
su mari su campagne inutilmente.

Mi abbandono all'amore di quei visi.

CITY

Ashen sunrise, I have no god.

Sleepy faces pass through the streets
buried under bundles of icy grass.
Vendors cry at the empty cold.

I once saw dawns more dense with color
on the sea and in the country—
what good was it?

I lose myself in the love of those faces.

FALSA PRIMAVERA

Placidi gatti, amanti
(sul prato l'ora è ferma)
di vetri luccicanti.

Goffamente beati,
da odore di caserma
si spogliano i soldati.

Ma effimero è alle cave
ansie il sole che ami.
Al vespro aspro, e grave
il cielo ai secchi rami.

FALSE SPRING

Quiet cats in love
(time stops on the grassy fields)
with shimmering panes.

Awkwardly blessed,
smelling of barracks,
the soldiers undress.

But the sun you love
doesn't last in the anxious quarries.
In the bitter evening, the sky
broods in the dry branches.

—PN 27

SERA NEL GIARDINO

La sera mi ha rapito
i rissosi fanciulli.
Le loro voci d'angeli
in guerra.
        Adesso in seno
a nuove luci stanno
là sull'opposte case.

Resta sul cielo chiaro
d'un eroe s'un cavallo
incisa macchia muta

sotto la prima stella.

SCUOLA

Negli azzurri mattini
le file svelte e nere
dei collegiali. Chini
su libri poi. Bandiere
di nostalgia campestre
gli alberi alle finestre.

EVENING IN THE PARK

The evening kidnapped
my quarreling boys.
Their angel voices
warring.
               Now they stand
in the mothering shelter of new lights
in houses across the street.

Engraved on the bright sky
the silent smudge
of a hero on a horse

under the first star.

SCHOOL

On blue mornings
the neat dark rows
of student boarders. Then
bent over their books. Trees
by the windows banners
calling them home.

— PN 27

Le nere scale della mia taverna
tu discendi tutto intriso di vento.
I bei capelli caduti tu hai
sugli occhi vivi in un mio firmamento
remoto.

Nella fumosa taverna
ora è l'odore del porto e del vento.
Libero vento che modella i corpi
e muove il passo ai bianchi marinai.

FAVOLA

In un salone in cui gridano gli ori
—sorpresi dalla luce dell'aprile—
un re ascolta cento e cento principi.

(Su vivi prati aleggiano taciuti
i canti . . . ? Poi festosamente arriva
il grido umano della ragazzaglia.)

Cadono voci e luci al vespro: frali
consistenze in aprile. Il re si perde
entro un lontano battere di ali.

All tangled with wind you walk
down the black stairs of my tavern.
Your lovely hair falls over your eyes
that quicken in my distant
heavens.

        The smoky tavern fills
with the smell of waterfront and wind.
Free wind shaping the bodies and
quickening the step of white sailors.

FABLE

In a great hall where golden things cry out
—surprised by the April light—
a king listens to hundreds of princes.

(What quiet songs quiver across
the greening fields? Louder now, festive,
the human cry of a bunch of kids.)

At sundown lights and voices dwindle, April's
frail consistencies. The king vanishes
in a distant flutter of wings.

FANTASIA PER UN INIZIO DI PRIMAVERA

I tuoi occhi infernali
non mi guardano più.
Sento nascere ali
in me. Già guardo in su.

Solcano verdi prati
leggeri treni neri
e scordano, beati,
le stazioni di ieri.
Ove—ferme le ore
su attoniti quadranti—
ritorna un vago amore
alle cose vaganti.

Partire è ancora lieve
se ti lasci alle spalle
—dimentico—la neve
che scende al fondo valle.

FANTASY FOR A SPRING BEGINNING

Your hellish eyes
no longer look at me.
I feel wings sprouting
in me. I'm already looking up.

Buoyant black trains
furrow green fields,
ecstatic to forget
yesterday's stations.
Here—hours stopped
on astonished clocks—
an uncertain love returns
to wandering things.

Leaving comes lightly
if you—forgetful—
turn your back on the snow
falling in the long valley.

Sotto il cielo di aprile la mia pace
è incerta. I verdi chiari ora si muovono
sotto il vento a capriccio. Ancora dormono
l'acque ma, sembra, come ad occhi aperti.

Ragazzi corrono sull'erba, e pare
che li disperda il vento. Ma disperso
solo è il mio cuore cui rimane un lampo
vivido (oh giovinezza) delle loro
bianche camicie stampate sul verde.

Under the April sky the peace I feel
is fitful. The bright greens sway
mindless in the wind. The water's
still asleep but seems, somehow, awake.

Kids are running on the grass as if
scattered by the wind. But it's only
this scattered heart of mine that holds a bright
flash (O youth) of their
white shirts printed on green.

IL BALCONE

Sorprendeva il fanciullo in avventure,
entro libri lontane, dalle ville
il monotono canto delle serve
—la noia verde della primavera.

Vuoti abbagli sul mare.
                  Ma la nera
lenta teoria dei seminaristi
sulla riva lontana disegnava
—ancora—vaste fantasie di viaggi.

Veleggiavano nuvole di marmo
dorate sullo spento monastero.
Ritornava dal cimitero, lieve,
nelle vie del paese un carro nero.

Le stelle sono immobili nel cielo.
L'ora d'estate è uguale a un'altra estate.
Ma il fanciullo che avanti a te cammina
se non lo chiami non sarà più quello . . .

THE BALCONY

The boy lost in adventures far away
inside his books, was surprised by the maids'
monotonous singing from the great houses—
the green boredom of spring.

Empty dazzle on the sea.
                              But the slow
black procession of schoolboys
on the distant shore sketched in—
again, again—huge fantasies of voyages.

Gilded marble clouds were running free
over the dead monastery.
Rolling lightly through the village streets,
a black wagon was coming from the cemetery.

The stars don't move in the sky,
the summer hour is like any other summer.
But the boy walking ahead of you—
if you don't speak up he'll never be the one . . .

Già mi parla l'autunno. Al davanzale
buio, tacendo, ascolto i miei pensieri
piegarsi sotto il vento occidentale
che scroscia sulle foglie dei miei neri
alberi solo vivi nella notte.
Poi mi chiudo nel letto. E mi saluta
il canto di un ragazzo che la notte,
immite, alleva: la vita non muta.

Esco dal mio lavoro tutto pieno
di aride parole. Ma al cancello
hanno posto gli dèi per la mia gioia
un fanciullo che giuoca con la noia.

Autumn speaks to me already. At the dark
window, silent, I listen to my thoughts
bending under the west wind
rippling the leaves of my black
trees, the only living things in the night.
Then I huddle in my bed. And I'm greeted
by the song of a boy brought up
by the pitiless night. Life doesn't change.

I leave my job filled
with dry words. But at the gate
the gods have set down for my joy
a boy playing with boredom.

Se sono vuoti gli alberi e il gennaio
comincia appena, a un puro sole brilla
sulla ghiaia del parco ora deserto
lo sputo del fanciullo ch'è passato
forse correndo mosso dall'aprile
lontano . . .

TORRE

Mi portano lontano
dal mondo le campane
del vespro. Ma le umane
trite cose? La mano
di quell'uomo al lavoro
su la spiaggia lontana
che già s'abbuia . . . Umana
tenerezza nel coro.

When the trees are bare and January
just beginning, a pure sun striking
the gravel in a deserted park
gleams in the spittle of a boy passing by,
maybe running, moved by far-off
April.

—PN 24

TOWER

The evening bells carry me
far away from
this world. But hackneyed
human things? The hand
of that man hard at work
on the distant beach
already turning dark . . . Human
tenderness in chorus.

Eccoli gli operai sul prato verde
a mangiare: non sono forse belli?
Corrono le automobili d'intorno,
passan le genti piene di giornali.

Ma gli operai non sono forse belli?

INTERNO

Dal portiere non c'era nessuno.
C'era la luce sui poveri letti
disfatti. E sopra un tavolaccio
dormiva un ragazzaccio
bellissimo.
        Uscì dalle sue braccia
annuvolate, esitando, un gattino.

Look at the workers on the green field
eating. Aren't they beautiful?
Cars drive by on every side,
people pass, clutching newspapers.

But the workers, aren't they beautiful?

INTERIOR

There was nobody in the porter's lodge.
Light glowed on miserable unmade
beds. And on a wooden board
slept a tough boy who was
very beautiful.
                    From his cloudy arms,
hesitating, leapt a kitten.

— PN 21

È pur dolce il ritrovarsi
per contrada sconosciuta.
Un ragazzo con la tuta
ora passa accanto a te.

Tu ne pensi alla sua vita
—a quel desco che l'aspetta.
E la stanca bicicletta
ch'egli posa accanto a sè.

Ma tu resti sulla strada
sconosciuta ed infinita.
Tu non chiedi alla tua vita
che restare ormai com'è.

It's also good to find yourself
on a sidestreet you don't know.
A boy in overalls
passes beside you.

You think about his life,
that rickety table waiting for him.
And the tired bicycle
he's walking at his side.

But you stay where you are
on that strange and infinite street.
All you ask of your life
is that it stay just as it is.

Era il settembre. Riandava la gente
rumorosa alle strade. Il sole amava
il vino e l'operaio. I canti ardevano
fino alla notte fonda.
                                    Ma restava
attonito un fanciullo, ormai legato
—sotto il caldo fogliame di una sera—
al ridere innocente di un amico . . .

IL VEGETALE

Lasciato ho gli animali con le loro
mille mutevoli inutili forme.
Respiro accanto a te, ora che annotta,
purpureo fiore sconosciuto: assai
meglio mi parli che le loro voci.
Dormi fra le tue verdi immense foglie,
purpureo fiore sconosciuto, vivo
come il lieve fanciullo che ho lasciato
dormire, un giorno, abbandonato all'erbe.

It was September. People walked
the noisy streets. The sun embraced
wine and worker. Songs burned
deep into the night.
                    But a boy stood there,
stunned, bound for the moment
—under the warm evening leafage—
to his friend's innocent laughter.

                              — PN 21

GREENERY

I've given up on animals with their
thousands of useless changing forms.
Now, at night, I breathe beside you,
unknown purple flower: you say
so much more to me than their voices.
Sleep among your huge green leaves,
strange purple flower, alive
as the gentle boy I left sleeping
one day, abandoned to the grass.

La veneta piazzetta,
antica e mesta, accoglie
odor di mare. E voli
di colombi. Ma resta
nella memoria—e incanta
di sè la luce—il volo
del giovane ciclista
vòlto all'amico: un soffio
melodico: "Vai solo?"

Io vivere vorrei addormentato
entro il dolce rumore della vita.

The small Venetian piazza,
old and mournful, welcomes
the sea-smell. And the pigeons
flying. But what stays
in memory—what enchants
the light—is a boy
flying by on a bicycle,
turning to his friend. A soft
whisper: "You alone?"

I'd like to live falling to sleep
inside all of life's sweet noise.

PAESAGGIO

La mattina di ottobre è ancora buia.
Seduto sovra un muro, un giovanotto
negli occhi ha il sonno ancora. D'improvviso
s'alza, saluta, grida un nome e viene
a lui correndo un fanciulletto lacero.
Questi saluta a pugni amorosissimi,
tira quegli alla mano e vuol giostrarlo.
Indi abbracciati vanno verso il bosco
sepolto fra le case popolari.

Ne usciranno soltanto al mezzogiorno
quando il sole gagliardo avrà disperso
quell'umida amicizia mattinale.

Mentre noi siamo qui, fra consuete
cose sepolti,—
                    è sul mondo la luna
e bagna il canto ai contadini. Quete
ascoltano le siepi.
                    Il fondo ascolto
della mia vita a quel lume di luna.

LANDSCAPE

The October morning is still dark.
The young boy sitting on the wall
still has sleep in his eyes. Suddenly
he stands up, waves, yells a name and a boy
with holes in his sleeves comes running.
They poke each other, jabbing affectionately;
one pulls the other's hand and wants to wrestle.
Then they walk arm in arm toward the woods
buried behind the housing project.

They won't come out until noon
when the robust sun has scattered
that moist morning friendship.

While we're here, buried among
the usual things,—
                        the moon's above the world
washing the peasants' song. Quietly
the bushes listen.
                        I listen
in that lunar light
to my life's deep center.

Le porte del mondo non sanno
che fuori la pioggia le cerca.
Le cerca. Le cerca. Paziente
si perde, ritorna. La luce
non sa della pioggia. La pioggia
non sa della luce. Le porte,
le porte del mondo son chiuse:
serrate alla pioggia,
serrate alla luce.

The doors of the world don't know
that the rain outside is searching.
Looking for them, for the doors. It slows,
biding time, returns. The light
doesn't know about the rain. The rain
doesn't know about the light. The doors,
the world's doors, are closed,
barred to the rain,
barred to the light.

I pini solitari lungo il mare
desolato non sanno del mio amore.
Li sveglia il vento, la pioggia
dolce li bacia, il tuono
lontano li addormenta.
Ma i pini solitari non sapranno
mai del mio amore, mai della mia gioia.

Amore della terra, colma gioia
incompresa. Oh dove porti
lontano! Un giorno
i pini solitari non vedranno
—la pioggia li lecca, il sole li addormenta—
coll'amore danzare la mia morte.

The solitary pines along the empty
sea know nothing of my love.
The wind wakes them, the soft
rain kisses them, the distant
thunder lulls them to sleep.
But the solitary pines will never know
about my love, never know my joy.

Love of the earth, overflowing
unconfined love. O what distance
is yours! One day
while the rain licks and sun brings sleep
the solitary pines won't see
my death dancing with love.

— PN 30

Era l'alba su i colli, e gli animali
ridavano alla terra i calmi occhi.
Io tornavo alla casa di mia madre.
Il treno dondolava i miei sbadigli
acerbi. E il primo vento era su l'erbe.

Altissimo e confuso, il paradiso
della mia vita non aveva ancora
volto. Ma l'ospite alla terra, nuovo,
già chiedeva l'amore, inginocchiato.

Cadeva la preghiera nella chiusa
casa entro odore di libri di scuola.
Navigavano al vespero felici
gridi di uccelli nel mio cielo d'ansia.

Dawn on the hills, and the animals
gave their steady eyes back to earth.
I was going home to my mother's house.
The train swayed, rocking my bitter
yawns. And the dawn wind was on the grass.

Exalted and confused, my life's
paradise had not yet reached
the turn. But the guest, new
and kneeling, asked the earth for love.

The prayer fell down into the closed
house, into the smell of schoolbooks.
At evening the joyous cries of birds
went sailing through my anxious sky.

Quando tornai al mare di una volta,
nella sera fra i caldi viali
ricercavo i compagni di allora . . .

Come un lupo impazzito odoravo
la calda ombra fra le case. L'odore
antico e vuoto mi cacciava all'ampia
spiaggia sul mare aperto. Lì trovavo
l'amarezza più chiara e la mia ombra
lunare ferma su l'antico odore.

LA TOMBA DEL PADRE

Cimitero nell'est. Un sole insiste
inutilmente sulla nuvolaglia.
Un ragazzo si stacca dalla mamma
e piscia verso il coro dei soldati
su i campi desolati lieto e triste.

When I went back to the sea I once knew
I searched the hot streets at night
for old friends and companions . . .

Like a crazed wolf, I went sniffing
the hot shadow between the houses. The old
empty smell drove me to the huge
beach by the open sea. It was there I found
my brightest bitterness and my moonlit
shadow standing on the old smell.

—PN 30

THE FATHER'S TOMB

Cemetery to the east. A sun beats
uselessly on the banks of clouds.
A boy leaves his mommy's side
and pisses toward the file of soldiers
on the desolate fields. He's happy, and sad.

—PN 27

FINE DI STAGIONE

Il mare chiaro e gaio
resta. Ma dove è andato
il bianco marinaio?

È la pineta assorta
nel sole. Ella ha varcato
come una chiusa porta

l'ingenua ferrovia.
E la pineta assorta
le tiene compagnia.

SEASON'S END

The sea's still bright
and gay. But where's
the white sailor gone?

The pines are absorbed
by the sun. They've crossed
over the innocent rails

as through a closed door.
And the pines, all absorbed,
keep the tracks company.

La luna di settembre su la buia
valle addormenta ai contadini il canto.

Una cadenza insiste: quasi lento
respiro di animale, nel silenzio,
salpa la valle se la luna sale.

Altro respira qui, dolce animale
anch'egli silenzioso. Ma un tumulto
di vita in me ripete antica vita.

Più vivo di così non sarò mai.

Quando la luce piange sulle strade
vorrei in silenzio un fanciullo abbracciare.

September moon on the dark valley
lulls to sleep the peasants' song.

A beat persists, a kind of slow
animal breathing in the silence,
lifting the valley when the moon rises.

Another breathing here, he too
a sweet, silent animal. But some upheaval
in me keeps repeating ancient life.

I will never be more alive than this.

— PN 26

When light weeps on the streets
I want to hug a boy in silence.

Un bicchiere di latte ed una piazza
col monumento. Un bicchiere di latte
dalle tue dolci sporche nuove mani.

Un giorno che alla terra abbandonavo
ogni calmo desio—e rispondeva calmo
il vento che dal mare risaliva
a noi del verde colle—
io nel sole un'umana figura
riguardavo dormire. Indi m'accorsi
che un vero iddio guardava quella forma.
Mi ritrassi in silenzio. Spaventato
fui nel dolce silenzio, azzurro mare.

A glass of milk and a piazza
with a statue. A glass of milk
from your sweet, new, dirty hands.

One day when I surrendered to the earth
all quiet passion—and the wind
rising from the sea to us
on the green hill gave quiet answer—
I watched a human form sleeping
in the sun. Then I realized
that a true god was watching that same form.
I withdrew in silence. In that sweet
silence, that blue sea, I was afraid.

—PN 26

Deserto è il fiume. E tu lo sai che basta
ora con le solari prodezze di ieri.
Bacio nelle tue ascelle, umidi, fieri,
gli odori di un'estate che si guasta.

Non era la città dove la sera
ebbro cantavo fra le sparse luci
sopra la dolce umidità del fiume.
Adesso un biondo sole sulla nera
bottega di mio padre par che bruci
la nostra assenza. E non ritrovo il fiume.

The river's deserted. And you know
that yesterday's sunlit exploits
are over. In your armpits I kiss
the fierce damp smells of a summer spoiling.

It wasn't the city where I used to sing
drunk at night among the scattered lights
above the sweet dampness of the river.
Now a blond sun over my father's black
store seems to burn away
our absence. And I can't find the river again.

LA SERA

Indi restammo in pochi—senza donne
nella campagna. Il freddo era cessato.
Ci guardammo in silenzio. Germinava
la terra. E il mio ragazzo ricordò: "L'altra stagione
ho guardato una donna—e tu dicevi:
'Chi ha sete nel sole
lasci la bicicletta
e aspetti la luna.'"

LA TEMPESTA

Fu in un dolce paese—ove estatica e verde
era la noia del meriggio al sole.
Venne un vento improvviso. E risalì dal verde
il dolce e rozzo amico dell'estate,
ma tutto caldo già, tutto vestito
—odoroso di stalla, fra le stelle
fitte fredde nel cielo.
Parlammo della mamma, e del giovane fuoco.
Di un caldo letto facemmo un bel giuoco.
Ma nel sonno riamammo le grotte.
Candido poi nel vento un fazzoletto
solitario brillava nella notte.

THE EVENING

Just a few of us were left—without women,
in the country. The air no longer cold.
We looked at each other in silence. The earth
swelled. And my boy remembered: "Last season
I looked at a woman and you said to me:
'If you're thirsty in sunlight
leave your bicycle
and wait for the moon.' "

THE TEMPEST

It was a sweet place, where noontime's sunny boredom
was ecstatic and green.
A sudden wind blew up. And my sweet rough
summer friend got up from the grass,
but already hot, completely dressed
—smelling of stables, among the stars
crowded cold in the sky.
We talked of his mom, and young fire.
We made a warm bed our playground.
But in sleep we fell in love with caves again.
Later, white in the wind, a lonely handkerchief
flashed in the night.

Non ami le pareti della tua
stanza. Hai negli occhi i papaveri rossi
in fuga. Il sorriso del giovane
acrobata. Il trionfo
di lui, o della tua
vita quando torna primavera.

Con un rapido vezzo hai liberato
la fronte dal ciuffetto. Fieramente
hai dato fuoco alla tua sigaretta.
Ma ricade il ciuffetto. E la stagione
indugia, e ride assai languidamente.

You don't love the walls of your
room. The red poppies growing in your eyes
blow away. The young acrobat's
smile. His triumph,
the triumph of your
life when spring comes back.

—PN 30

One neat flick freed your
forehead of hair. You lighted
your cigarette proudly.
But the hair falls back. And the season
lingers, laughing very softly.

Era per la città quasi un comune
personaggio, sebbene assai gentile.
E tale fu nel tram. Lento rossore
appariva e spariva. Lentamente
fummo portati a una dolce deriva.
Moriva il giorno alla periferia.

Indi lo vidi con il suo segreto
di carne allontanarsi, personaggio
anonimo rientrare nell'amico
cielo dell'alba, a sera. Era il suo velo
fra le mie mani: il rossore di un rudere antico.

Viene l'alba d'estate. Oh prima luce
sul letto del fratello. Nel silenzio
la ferma confusione: panni e sesso.
Quando viene l'estate lascia questo
malinconico ardore. Nel silenzio
raggiungi il mare placido di luce.

In the city he seemed an ordinary
sort of person, though very kind.
As he was in the streetcar. Slow blush
spreading and fading. Slowly
we drifted away together.
The day was dying on the city's edge.

Then I saw him move away
with his secret of flesh, a nameless
figure walking back into the dawn's
friendly sky, at evening. It was his veil
I held in my hands: the blush of an ancient ruin.

— PN 26

The summer dawn rises. O early light
on my brother's bed. In the silence
all confusion stilled: sheets and sex.
When summer comes, leave behind this
unhappy passion. In the silence
go back to the serene sea of light.

La mia vita è monotona, se arde
un calmo sole alle persiane verdi.
Si fa docile sguardo, calmo amore
anonimo, poesia di quattro versi.

La semplice poesia forse discende
distratta come cala al viaggiatore
entro l'arida folla di un convoglio
la mano sulla spalla di un ragazzo.

Malinconia d'amore, dove resta
bianco il sorriso del fanciullo come
un ultimo gabbiano alla tempesta.

My life is monotonous when quiet
sunlight scorches the green shutters.
It becomes a passive glance, quiet
nameless love, a four-line poem.

Maybe plain and easy poetry happens
unthinking as a traveler's hand
inside an airless crowded train
falling on a boy's shoulder.

Love's sadness, where the boy's
laughter stays white as
the last gull in a storm.

L'insonnia delle rondini. L'amico
quieto a salutarmi alla stazione.

L'accusato non ha se non parole.
E talvolta non ha, anzi non vuole
sotto il sole le sole parole.

Immobile nel sole la campagna
pareva riascoltare il suo segreto.
Un giovane passò ma non so ancora
se vero oppure vivo come fiamma
che il sole riassorbiva nel silenzio.

The swallows' insomnia. My quiet
friend greeting me at the station.

The accused has only words.
And sometimes he doesn't have, or even want,
only sunlit words in sunlight.

Motionless in sunlight, the landscape
seemed to be listening to its own secret.
A young man went by but I still don't know
if he was real or alive as a flame
reabsorbed by sunlight in silence.

Forse invecchio, se ho fatto un lungo viaggio
sempre seduto, se nulla ho veduto
fuor che la pioggia, se uno stanco raggio
di vita silenziosa . . . (gli operai
pigliavano e lasciavano il mio treno,
portavano da un borgo a un dolce lago
il loro sonno coi loro utensili).
Quando giunsi nel letto anch'io gridai:
uomini siamo, più stanchi che vili.

Maybe I'm getting old, staying seated
the whole long journey, seeing nothing outside
but the rain, and a tired sunbeam
of silent life . . . (workmen
climbed on and off my train,
carrying their sleep with their tools
from a small town to a quiet lake).
When I reached my bed I too cried out:
we're men, we're tired, not wretched.

Qualcuno vi parlava e voi rispondevate
sullo strano argomento delle vendite a rate.
Poi d'un tratto—chiudeste gli occhi per un momento
come per rivedere—e d'un fiato: chi era
intorno a una fontana, solitario e di sera?
C'era allora la guerra, è vero, e c'era il coprifuoco,
ma fuggir spaventato per un soldato ignoto!
Forse non era un'ombra, quell'uomo, era un fanciullo
e la sua fuga un giuoco soltanto volontario.
E riprendeste il corso del discorso interrotto.
Ma d'un tratto affondaste in un pianto dirotto.
Così tra i chiari affari la ria malinconia
s'introduce vestita di buia nostalgia.

Abbandonarsi all'onda delle sensazioni
come quest'acqua bionda che si smorza
e si riaccende sotto un giallo sole
carico, come me, di umiliazione.

Someone was talking to you and you were answering
with a strange remark about installment plans.
Then suddenly—you shut your eyes for an instant
as if reconsidering—and in a breath: Who was it
beside the fountain, alone, at night?
The war was still on, yes, and there was a curfew,
but to run away terrified by a strange soldier!
Maybe he wasn't a shadow, that man, but just
a boy and his running away merely a game of his own.
And you picked up the broken thread of the conversation.
But suddenly you collapsed into wild tears.
The way a stream of sadness, dressed in dark
nostalgia, slips in when things are sharp and clear.

— PN 24

Surrendering to the wave of feelings
like this blond water that smothers
then rekindles under a yellow sun
loaded, like me, with humiliation.

Amavo ogni cosa nel mondo. E non avevo
che il mio bianco taccuino sotto il sole.

Lumi del cimitero, non mi dite
che la sera d'estate non è bella.
E belli sono i bevitori dentro
le lontane osterie.

Muovonsi come fregi
antichi sotto il cielo
nuovo di stelle.

Lumi del cimitero, calmi diti
contano lente sere. Non mi dite
che la notte d'estate non è bella.

I loved everything in the world. And all I had
was my small blank notebook in the sunlight.

Cemetery lights, don't tell me
the summer night isn't beautiful.
And beautiful too are the drinkers
in faraway taverns.

Stirring like an ancient
frieze under a sky
fresh with stars.

Cemetery lights, peaceful fingers
count slow evenings. Don't tell me
the summer night isn't beautiful.

—PN 21

Ero solo nel mondo, o il mondo aveva
un segreto per me? Di primavera
mi svegliavo a un monotono accordo
e il canto di un amore mi pareva.
Il canto di un amore che premeva
con gli occhi di quel cielo puro e fermo.

Sedere a una tavola ignota.
Dormire in un letto non mio.
Sentire la piazza già vuota
gonfiarsi in un tenero addio.

I was alone in the world, or did the world
hold some secret for me? In spring
I woke to a single harmonious note
that seemed to me a song of love.
The love song pressing down
with the eyes of that pure, still sky.

To sit at a strange table.
To sleep in a bed that isn't mine.
To feel the empty piazza
swell in a tender goodbye.

Ditemi, grandi alberi sognanti,
a voi non batte il cuore quando amore
fa cantar la cicala, quando il sole
sorprende e lascia immobile nel tempo
il batticuore alla tenera lucertola
perduta fra due mani in un dolce far niente?
Anche a me batte il cuore, e pur non sono
io del fanciullo vittima innocente.

Ero solo e seduto. La mia storia
appoggiavo a una chiesa senza nome.
Qualche figura entrò senza rumore,
senz'ombra sotto il cielo del meriggio.

Nude campane che la vostra storia
non raccontate mai con precisione.
In me si fabbricò tutto il meriggio
intorno ad una storia senza nome.

Tell me, you great dreaming trees,
doesn't your heart beat when love
makes the cicada sing, when the sun
surprises and suspends in time
the heartbeat of a tender lizard
vanishing between two hands idly playing?
My heart too starts beating, even though
I'm not that boy's innocent victim.

— PN 26

I was sitting alone. I entrusted
the story of my life to a nameless church.
A few figures entered quietly,
shadowless under the noontime sky.

You naked bells, you never tell
your story exactly as it is.
In me the noontime invented itself
entirely, around a nameless history.

L'estate se ne andò senza rumore.
Nubi leggere ad una ad una il cuore
gremirono di segni senza nome.
La luna trascorreva ansiosa e onesta.

Lunga distesa sovra un muro nella
canicola dormiva un'altra età.
Nella mano stringeva il suo più caro
oggetto. Non per pudore chè non ha pudore
il sonno, e il sogno è solo anche in città.

Un uomo già cantava nel suo buio
e il figlio l'ascoltava sulla riva
del mare, nel silenzio, accanto a un sasso.
Noi gli chiedemmo di farci vedere,
era l'alba, il suo bianco silenzio.
Poi ce ne andammo con il cuore in gola
ridendo e incespicando ad ogni passo.

Summer made no noise when it left.
Clouds drifting one by one crammed
my heart with nameless signs.
The anxious honest moon passed overhead.

Another age, sprawled full-length
in dogstar heat, was sleeping on the wall.
In his hand he clutched his most precious
object. Not from shame—sleep feels no shame—
and even in the city dreaming goes alone.

A man was singing in his darkness
and his son listened to him on the shore
of the sea, in silence, beside a rock.
We asked him to show us,
at dawn, his white silence.
Then we left, hearts in our throats,
laughing and stumbling at every step.

Il treno tarderà di almeno un'ora.
L'acqua del mare si fa più turchina.
Sul muro calcinato il campanello
casalingo non suona. La panchina
di ferro scotta al sole. Le cicale
sono le sole padrone dell'ora.

The train will be at least an hour late.
The blue-green of the water darkens.
The doorbell on the whitewashed wall
doesn't ring. The iron
bench burns in the sun. The cicadas
are sole masters of the hour.

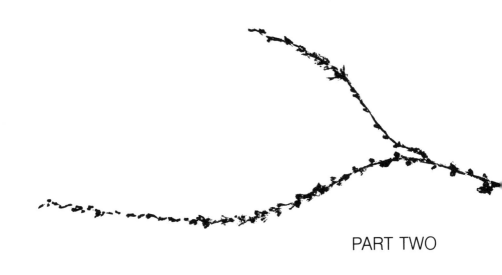

PART TWO

Felice chi è diverso
essendo egli diverso.
Ma guai a chi è diverso
essendo egli comune.

E poi son solo. Resta
la dolce compagnia
di luminose ingenue bugie.

Happy the man who is different,
happy being different.
But God help the man who is
ordinary but different.

— PN 24

And so I'm alone. Alone
in the gentle company
of shining innocent lies.

Viaggiava per la terra
come un giovane Iddio
colui che non aveva
amori sulla terra.
Tornava dalla festa
la giovane animale
molti colori in testa
e frutti nel grembiale.

Non è la timidezza che tu celi forse un sogno
confuso degli dèi?

He walked the earth
like a young god
who had no
loves on earth.
The young animal
returned from the festival,
his head bursting with colors,
his apron heavy with fruit.

— PN 30

Isn't the shyness you hide perhaps a puzzled
dream of the gods?

Qui è la cara città dove la notte
alta non ti spaura. Amici
solitari qui passano e ti danno
uno sguardo d'amore. O tu lo credi . . .

Il fanciullo magretto torna a casa
un poco stanco e molto interessato
alle cose dell'autobus. Pensa
—con quella luce che viene dai sensi
dai sensi ancora appena appena tocca—
in quanti modi adoperar si possa
una cosa ch'è nuova e già non tiene
se inavvertito ogni tanto egli tocca.
Poi si accorge di me. E raffreddato
si soffia il cuore fra due grosse mani.

Io devo scendere ed è forse un bene.

This is the good city where the dead
of night never scares you. Solitary
friends pass by giving you a loving
glance. Or so you think . . .

— PN 30

A skinny young boy is on his way home,
a little tired but fascinated
by things in the bus. He thinks
—with that light coming from the senses,
light still just barely touching—
of all the ways to use something new,
something that won't take hold
though sometimes he touches it unknowingly.
Then he notices me. Suddenly chilled,
he blows on his heart in his two large hands.

I have to get off and it's probably just as well.

— PN 24

Un po' di pace è già nella campagna.
L'ozio che è il padre dei miei sogni guarda
i miei vizi coi suoi occhi leggeri.

Qualcuno che era in me ma me non guarda
bagna e si mostra negligente: appare
d'un tratto un treno coi suoi passeggeri
attoniti e ridenti: ed è già ieri.

Dacci la gioia di conoscer bene
le nostre gioie, con le nostre pene.

There's still a little peace in the country.
The idleness fathering all my dreams looks
at my vices with gentle eyes.

Someone who was in me isn't looking now:
he goes in swimming, unconcerned. Suddenly
a train appears, its passengers shocked
and laughing. And it's now yesterday.

Grant us the joy of knowing well
our joys, and our sufferings.

Se l'inverno comincia sulle calde
e sporche mani un odore di arance
al quieto sole della festa arde
nell'aria come qualcosa che piange.

Un dì la vita mia era beata.
Tutta tesa all'amore anche un portone
rifugio per la pioggia era una gioia.
Anche la pioggia mi era alleata.

Winter begins and a smell
of oranges on warm dirty hands
in the calm holiday sun
burns in the air like something crying.

My life one day was blessed.
Everything tensed toward love, even a doorway
shelter in the rain was bliss.
Even the rain was with me.

—PN 30

Con il cielo coperto e con l'aria monotona
grassa di assenti rumori lontani
nella mia età di mezzo (nè giovane nè vecchia)
nella stagione incerta, nell'ora più chiara
cosa venivo io a fare con voi sassi e barattoli vuoti?
L'amore era lontano o era in ogni cosa?

Come è forte il rumore dell'alba!
Fatto di cose più che di persone.
Lo precede talvolta un fischio breve,
una voce che lieta sfida il giorno.
Ma poi nella città tutto è sommerso.
E la mia stella è quella stella scialba
mia lenta morte senza disperazione.

With the sky overcast and the bleak flat air
fat with absent faraway sounds
in my middle age (neither young nor old)
in the shifting season, in the brightest instant
what had I to do with you stones and tin cans?
Was love far away or in every last thing?

Dawn makes so much noise!
Of things more than people.
Sometimes a brief whistle comes first,
a happy voice defying the day.
But then the whole city goes under.
And my star is that fading star,
my slow dying, without desperation.

Mi ridestava la voce
del giovane operaio che cantava
dentro la stanza vuota.

Sul campo aperto giuocano al pallone.
Il sole ora l'investe ora li lascia.
La camera d'albergo è del mio corpo
nudo agli specchi. E sconosciuta
è la città.

I was roused again
by the voice of the young worker singing
in the empty room.

—PN 24

They're playing ball on the wide field.
The sun pounds them, leaves them.
The hotel room belongs to my body
naked in the mirrors. I don't know
what city I'm in.

È bello lavorare
nel buio di una stanza
con la testa in vacanza
lungo un azzurro mare.

Se desolato io cammino . . . dietro
quel soffio di colline, nella notte
tepida e buia, steso su una zolla
è forse un giovanetto ad occhi aperti.

Ognuno è solo, ma con vario cuore
riguarda sempre le solite stelle.

It's good to work
in the dark of a room
with your mind on holiday
beside a blue sea.

— PN 30

If I go for a walk, dejected . . . behind
that breath of hills, in the dark
muggy night, there may be a boy
lying on the broken ground, his eyes open.

Everyone's alone, we look at the same
old stars, always, yet the feeling's different.

— PN 24

Sole con luna, mare con foreste,
tutt'insieme baciare in una bocca.

Ma il ragazzo non sa. Corre a una porta
di triste luce. E la sua bocca è morta.

"Lasciami andare se già spunta l'alba."
Ed io mi ritrovai solo fra i vuoti
capanni interminabili sul mare.
Fra gli anonimi e muti cubi anch'io
cercavo una dimora? Il mare, il chiaro
mare non mi voltò con la sua luce? Salva
era soltanto la malinconia?
L'alba mi riportò, stanca, una via.

Sun with moon, sea with forests,
everything kissing, all one mouth.

But the boy doesn't know it. He runs
toward a door's sad light. And his mouth is dead.

"Let me go, it's nearly dawn."
And I found myself alone again among
the endless empty cabins by the sea.
Was I too looking for a place to live
among those nameless, unspeaking cubicles?
Didn't the sea, the bright sea, change me
with its light? Everything except my sadness?
The weary dawn opened one way back for me.

—PN 24

Amico, sei lontano. E la tua vita
ha intorno a sé colori ch'io non vedo.
Ha la mia vita intorno a sé colori
che io non vedo.

DONNA IN TRAM

Vuoi baciare il tuo bimbo che non vuole:
ama guardare la vita, di fuori.
Tu sei delusa allora, ma sorridi:
non è l'angoscia della gelosia
anche se già somiglia egli all'altr'uomo
che per "guardare la vita, di fuori"
ti ha lasciata così . . .

Friend, you're far away. And your life
swarms with colors I can't see.
My own life swarms with colors
I can't see.

WOMAN IN A STREETCAR

You try to kiss your boy, but he refuses.
He loves to watch what's going on outside.
You're disappointed but smile anyway.
Your sorrow isn't jealousy
even though he already resembles another man
who wanted "to watch what's going on outside"
and left you as you are . . .

— PN 27

Nel chiuso lago, sola, senza vento
la mia nave trascorre, ad ora ad ora.
Fremono i fiori sotto i ponti. Sento
la mia tristezza accendersi ancora.

Guarirai. Si odono i treni
lontani,—e la città notturna
perde la tramontana
operosa, e si addorme
un attimo in attesa
di un vento di campane.

My boat drifts, windless, alone,
hour after hour on the narrow lake.
The flowers quiver under the bridges. I feel
my old sadness kindling again.

You'll recover. You can hear the trains
in the distance. And the city night
sheds the toiling
north wind and for a moment
drifts asleep waiting
for the wind-borne bells.

Lungo è il tragitto in autobus. Anche
se la campagna fuori è così bella.
Anzi sognata tra la nebbia. Un rozzo
garzone di fornaio una sua tenera
grazia concede ad attimi e poi nega
facendo di quel tratto una catena
di bei ricordi da sgranare a sera.

Amore, gioventù, liete parole,
cosa splende su voi e vi dissecca?
Resta un odore come merda secca
lungo le siepi cariche di sole.

The bus trip's long. Even though
the countryside's so beautiful.
Like a dream in the fog. A rough
baker's boy now and then offers one
of his soft graces, then pulls back,
making those moments a chain of lovely
memories to be plucked at night.

—PN 24

Love, youth, sweet words,
what shines on you, what shrivels you?
An odor remains like the smell of dry dung
along the hedgerows drenched with sun.

La mia poesia non sarà
un giuoco leggero
fatto con parole delicate
e malate
(sole chiaro di marzo
su foglie rabbrividenti
di platani di un verde troppo chiaro).
La mia poesia lancerà la sua forza
a perdersi nell'infinito
(giuochi di un atleta bello
nel vespero lungo d'estate).

Il fanciullo che ascolta nei libri
canti di amori perduti
non ne capisce niente. Guarda
guarda un vetro sul tetto
riluccicare forte
in un tramonto acceso . . .
Si china poi sulla sua carne, come
su di un bianco diario.

My poetry won't be
a breezy game
made of fragile
sickly words
(bright March sun
on the quivering leaves
of sycamores too green in the light).
My poetry will hurl its strength
and lose itself in the infinite
(games of a handsome athlete
in the long summer evening).

The boy listening to songs
of lost love in his books
doesn't understand a thing. He looks,
looks at a window on the roof
shining brightly
in a blazing sunset.
Then he hunches over his flesh, as
over a blank diary.

Mi adagio nel mattino
di primavera. Sento
nascere in me scomposte
aurore. Io non so più
se muoio o pure nasco.

Voglio credere ancora in te, Marcello.
Anche se il mondo a me ti fa lontano.
Voglio credere ancora alla tua mano
amichevole, al tuo sorriso, a quello
che destano i tuoi occhi nel mio cuore.
Se partono soldati per la guerra
cantando—e il canto i nostri cuori serra,
diversi—ride fra noi due amore.

I lie down in the spring
morning. I feel
disordered dawns sprouting
inside me. I no longer know
whether I'm dying or being born.

I want to go on believing in you, Marcello.
Even if the world keeps us apart.
I want to go on believing in your friendly
hand, your smile, in whatever
your eyes awaken in my heart.
When soldiers go off to the war
singing—their singing twists our hearts,
differently—love laughs between the two of us.

—PN 30

Vivere è per amare qualche cosa.
Oggi è il fanciullo che ha rubato un paio
di scarpe a quel signore arrogantissimo.

Ho difeso il fanciullo. L'ho salvato
da chi sa quale buio. (Il bel fanciullo
che ruba i cani belli per amarli).

MATTINO

grigiastro e secco. Ad una sporca corda
vinto è un cavallo—e non sa più se c'era
verde sui prati. Un ragazzino piscia
contro un albero magro—e corre via.

Il malato moriva. Per la strada
un ciclista batteva contro un uomo.
Cadevano i biscotti. Li mangiava
ugualmente un ragazzo—e poi correva.

We live to love something.
Today it's the boy who stole a pair
of shoes from an incredibly arrogant man.

I defended the boy. I saved him
from some kind of darkness. (The beautiful boy
who steals beautiful dogs so he can love them.)

MORNING

pale gray and parched. A horse tied down
by a dirty rope—he can't tell anymore
if the fields were ever green.
A young boy pisses against a spindly tree
then runs away.

The sick man was dying. A cyclist
ran into a man on the street.
Cookies fell. A boy
ate them anyway, then ran off.

L'ombra di una nuvola leggera
mi condusse a un fanciullo
che uscito dal torrente
nudo si stese sull'erba.
                    Mi sentii
come dopo la prima comunione.

                    E su di lei
rotolarono giorni verdi e uguali
e monotoni vespri con le donne
ferme sugli usci di vie desolate
a manovrare pettini e capelli.

Di febbraio a Milano
non c'erano le nebbie.
Ma numerosi sciami di ciclisti
andavano nel sole silenziosi.
E li fermava come in una gara
sospesa il suonatore siciliano.

The shadow of a drifting cloud
led me to a boy
who climbed from the river
and lay naked on the grass.
                                    I felt
as I did after my first communion,

                                    and over it
green days rolled, all alike,
and monotonous nights with women
standing by doors on desolate streets
adjusting their hair and combs.

That February in Milan
there wasn't any fog.
But swarms of bicyclists
wheeled silent in the sun.
Suddenly stopped, as in a race
suspended, by the Sicilian musician.

                    — PN 24

Tutto il giorno passai coi contadini.
Altro non feci che vederli fare.
La sera la vergogna ai colmi vini
mi prese: alla taverna cosa stavo io a fare?

Isolato, in un angolo, oh sul muro
leggo atterrito e attratto: "il nostro Sandro
poeta fa l'amore di sicuro,
è sempre solo muto come un mulo."
Senza fiato rimango, ormai felice
di quel che il muro, a me tacendo, dice.

Indifeso fervore. Brilla sul ciglio
lungo del popolano il *varietà*.
Ognuno è nel suo cuore un immortale.

I spent all day with the peasants.
I didn't do a thing, I just watched them work.
At night the shame of too much wine
seized me—what was I doing in the tavern?

Alone, in a corner, I read, with terror
and delight, on the wall: "Our poet
Sandro really does make love,
he's always alone, dumb like a mule."
I can't breathe, I'm happy now
with what the wall, unspeaking, says.

—PN 24

Unguarded passion. Burlesque glamor
glows on the long eyelash
of the common man.
At heart everyone's an immortal.

MORALISTI

Il mondo che vi pare di catene
tutto è tessuto d'armonìe profonde.

Sempre fanciulli nelle mie poesie!
Ma io non so parlare d'altre cose.
Le altre cose son tutte noiose.
Io non posso cantarvi Opere Pie.

Oh il lamento arrugginito
di un rimorso troppo antico
dai camini nel silenzio
della notte sotto il vento.

MORALISTS

The world that you see made of chains
is woven throughout with deepset harmonies.

Always boys in my poems!
But I can't talk about anything else.
Everything else bores me.
I can't sing you Salvation Army songs.

— PN 24

O the sad rusty song
of some ancient regret
from chimneys in the silence
of night on the wind.

Fuoco nero fra schiuma di mare
i tuoi occhi, confusi in un sogno
di viaggio e solitudine, mio amore.

Sempre affacciato a una finestra io sono,
io della vita tanto innamorato.
Unir parole ad uomini fu il dono
breve e discreto che il cielo mi ha dato.

Black fire on sea foam
your eyes floundering in a dream
of travel and solitude, my love.

I'm always standing by a window,
always so much in love with life.
Joining words to men was the brief
adequate gift the gods gave me.

— PN 30

Imbruna l'aria, e il lume
del giorno a lui dintorno
lentissimo si chiude.

Ma su l'umido fiume
cadono lente voci
di uccelli. Su la via
dilagano festosi
saluti sconosciuti
nei fischi dei ciclisti.

Gli invisibili treni
entro lucidi appelli
stasera non avranno
la sua malinconia.

The air darkens and daylight
very slowly closes
around him.

But bird voices fall
softly on the misty
river. The street
floods with happy
unfamiliar greetings,
the whistles of bicycle riders.

The trains invisible
inside shimmering appeals
will not share
his sadness tonight.

— PN 30

Sulla riva del fiume ancora brillano
nudi corpi di uomini lontani.

Qui la scena ha un grembiule nero. Strillano,
frammiste come sono ai loro cani,
le operaie che lasciano il lavoro.
Saranno forse sceme ma la loro
gioia frutterà come un buon seme.

IL VIAGGIO

Su coste desolate si batteva
il luminoso mare. In alto lievi
paesi: lievi spoglie sotto il sole.
(Sotto il sole medesimo gli antichi
abitatori.) Io siedo all'osteria
nella nuova città. Rientro dove il sole
brilla sereno sugli oggetti, e ride
il vecchio mendicante al suo giovane cane.

Bodies of naked men in the distance
are shining on the riverbank.

The scene here is aproned in black. Women
leaving work, all jumbled together,
yell to their dogs.
They may be silly, but their joy
will bear fruit like any good seed.

THE JOURNEY

The shining sea pounded
the desolate shore. High above, fragile
villages: fragile ruins in the sunlight.
(In the same sunlight its ancient
inhabitants.) I'm sitting in the tavern
in the new town. I'm back where the sunlight
shines serenely on things, where
the old beggar laughs at his puppy.

—PN 31

ALLA LUNA

A te che chiaro hai il volto il mio nascondo.
All'ombra di un grande albero che appena
mi copre, appena copre il mio tumulto.
Felicità o dolore, o forse solo
l'ombra di un cane o di un fanciullo ancora
che restare non vogliono animali.

PIANTO

Da un grande casamento,
pieno di luci, viene
solo un rumore, assurdo
e inutile, di latta.

L'infanzia, se rammento,
è a volte un poco sciatta.

TO THE MOON

From your bright face I hide my own.
In the shade of a great tree that barely
covers me, barely covers my torment.
Happiness or sorrow, or maybe just
the shadow of a dog or yet another boy
who want no more to be animals.

CRYING

From a large tenement
decked with lights comes
a single sound, absurd,
pointless, tinny.

Childhood, I remember,
is sometimes a little messy.

Voi già sognate il caffelatte. Io la mia tazza
l'ho già bevuta. Ora mi aspetta
la fredda stanza
con le lenzuola
ancora calde
dell'operaio, che per le scale
m'incontrerà
con quello sguardo
di chi non sa
ma molto sa.

"Poeta esclusivo d'amore"
m'hanno chiamato. E forse era vero.
Ma il vento qui sull'erba ed i rumori
della città lontana
non sono anch'essi amore?
Sotto nuvole calde
non sono ancora i suoni
di un amore che arde
e più non si allontana?

While you're still dreaming of your morning coffee
I've already had my cup. Now the chilly room
is waiting for me,
its bedsheets
still warm
from the worker who will meet me
on the stairs
with that look of someone
who doesn't know
but knows so much.

—PN 30

"A love poet exclusively"
they've called me. And maybe it was true.
But the wind here in the grass and the sounds
of the city in the distance
are love too, aren't they?
Under warm clouds
can't you still hear sounds
of a love that burns
and will not leave?

Talvolta, camminando per la via
non t'è venuto accanto a una finestra
illuminata dire un nome, o notte?
Rispondeva soltanto il tuo silenzio.
Ma le stelle brillavano ugualmente.
E il mio cuore batteva per me solo.

Alfio che un treno porta assai lontano.
Dove porti i tuoi occhi dolorosi
e tanto lieti insieme? Adesso è l'alba
e già tanto lontana pare la sera
che da poco è trascorsa con noi. La sera
in cui non hai voluto darmi
quello che solo meritavo, quello
che non dato m'incendia cuore e mente
a tal punto che l'alba o la sera od il giorno
fanno una confusione
in cui vedo soltanto il tuo lume.

Sometimes, walking down a street,
passing a bright window,
haven't you felt the urge
to speak a name, O night?
Only your silence answered.
But the stars shone all the same.
And my heart beat for me alone.

A train taking Alfio far away.
Where are you taking your eyes, at once
so bright and sorrowful? It's dawn now,
and the night that we just spent together
now seems so far away. The night
in which you didn't want to give me
what I alone deserved and which,
ungiven, fires my heart and mind
so much that dawn and night and day
become a pure confounding
in which I see only your light.

Non c'è più quella grazia fulminante
ma il soffio di qualcosa che verrà.

CRONACHE DI PRIMAVERA

Il primo uomo
nudo, al mattino sul greto del fiume
rabbrividiva ancora. Amore, a sera,
tormentava la donna che il fanciullo,
meraviglioso, abbandonava: il vivido
gesto di lui io vidi entro una buia
strada protesa alla campagna: amici
gli erano i nuovi campi e il sole—i lunghi
gridi dei treni nella notte accesi.

No more of that lightning grace
but the breath of something soon to be.

SPRING NEWS

                          The first man
naked, at morning on the pebbly river bank,
was still shivering. Love, at evening,
tortured the woman whom the boy,
the magical boy, was leaving. I saw
his lively motion on a dark street
stretching into the country. His friends
were the fresh fields and sun—the long
wail of trains blazing into the night.

                    — PN 31

Forse sull'erba verde un dì nasceva
la mia storia segreta: estremi ardori
di un sobborgo in vacanza.
Pioggia da gonfie nubi silenziosa.
Luci della città sulla campagna vuota.

E poi come una mosca
impigliata nel miele . . .

I think my secret story was born one day
on the green grass: passionate loves
in a quiet summer suburb.
Silent rain from swollen clouds.
City lights on the empty countryside.

And then like a fly
stuck in honey . . .

— PN 24